on th
Transformation
Wargame 2000

Walter Perry

Bruce Pirnie

John Gordon IV

Louis Moore

Robert Howe

Daniel R. Gonzales

David Johnson

Prepared for the United States Army

Arroyo Center

RAND

The research described in this report was sponsored by the United States Army under Contract No. DASW01-01-C-0003.

Library of Congress Cataloging-in-Publication Data

A report on the Army Transformation Wargame 2000 / Walter Perry ... [et al.].
    p. cm.
    "MR-1335."
    Includes bibliographical references.
    ISBN 0-8330-3061-2
    1. War games. 2. United States. Army—Reorganization. I. Perry, Walter, 1940–

    U310 .R47 2001
    355.4'8—dc21

                                           2001048341

RAND is a nonprofit institution that helps improve policy and decisionmaking through research and analysis. RAND® is a registered trademark. RAND's publications do not necessarily reflect the opinions or policies of its research sponsors.

Published 2001 by RAND
1700 Main Street, P.O. Box 2138, Santa Monica, CA 90407-2138
1200 South Hayes Street, Arlington, VA 22202-5050
201 North Craig Street, Suite 102, Pittsburgh, PA 15213
RAND URL: http://www.rand.org/
To order RAND documents or to obtain additional information, contact Distribution Services: Telephone: (310) 451-7002;
Fax: (310) 451-6915; Email: order@rand.org

The U.S. Army Training and Doctrine Command (TRADOC) conducted the Army Transformation Wargame 2000 (ATWG 2000) to support the Army Chief of Staff's vision for the future Army—one able to attain strategic dominance across the entire spectrum of operations. TRADOC's Deputy Chief of Staff for Doctrine (DCSDOC) requested that RAND support this effort.

This report presents RAND's analysis of ATWG 2000. It identifies issues that emerged from these activities and briefly explores implications. This report should be of interest to Army force designers interested in examining the future role of land forces.

This research was sponsored by TRADOC's DCSDOC and conducted in the Strategy, Doctrine, and Resources Program of RAND Arroyo Center. The Arroyo Center is a federally funded research and development center sponsored by the United States Army. Comments and inquiries should be addressed to Walter Perry, at Walter_Perry@rand.org or (703) 413-1100.

For more information on RAND Arroyo Center, contact the Director
of Operations (tel 310-393-0411, extension 6500; FAX 310-451-6952;
e-mail donnab@rand.org), or visit the Arroyo Center's Web site at
http://www.rand.org/organization/ard/.

CONTENTS

FIGURES

The Training and Doctrine Command (TRADOC)–sponsored Army Transformation Wargame 2000 (ATWG 2000) was held at the Army War College in Carlisle, Pennsylvania, from April 30 to May 5, 2000. The game had three purposes: (1) to support the Army Transformation to the Objective Force, (2) to provide a visualization of the future strategic and operational environment for this force, and (3) to facilitate understanding of the Army vision.[1]

SCENARIOS

ATWG 2000 was a free-play, two-sided, operational-level, seminar-wargame conducted in three independent vignettes. The vignettes were independent in that decisions made during the preceding vignette did not affect the situation at the start of the next one. The vignettes covered crisis response, warfighting, and post-conflict operations.

The scenario was set in Southwest Asia in the 2015 time frame. The New Independent Republic (NIR) composed of the former Iraq and Iran threatened Turkey and Syria over water rights to the Tigris and Euphrates rivers. The United States entered the conflict on the side of North Atlantic Treaty Organization (NATO) ally Turkey to defend it and its neighbor, Syria, against an invasion by the NIR.

---

[1]U.S. Army Training and Doctrine Command (TRADOC), *Army Transformation Wargame 2000, Game Book*, Fort Monroe, Va., 2000d.

GAME STRUCTURE

The structure of the game is illustrated in Figure S.1. The Operational Insights Panels consisted of two Blue-Red pairs and focused on the vignettes. Each of these pairs was presented with different vignettes within the context of the same scenario. The Operational Insights Panels produced plans (Red and Blue) as a result of the vignettes presented to them and the concept of operations prepared during the March 2000 Military Planning Seminar.[2] During ATWG 2000, each panel played a two-sided seminar wargame, thus allowing consideration of two different cases.

The Strategic Insights Panel had oversight of both cases and consisted of functional area specialists. During each vignette, their mission was to consider a set of issues within the context of the vignette

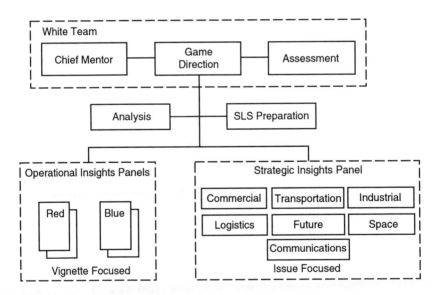

Figure S.1—ATWG 2000 Game Structure

---

[2]The Military Planning Seminar was designed to produce concept plans for both Red and Blue forces. The seminar was held in Washington, D.C., from March 14 to 17, 2000.

and develop issues and insights not directly associated with the vignettes. Team members were free to visit the Operational Insights Panels during their deliberations to gain an understanding of operational issues. RAND both observed game play and participated in the deliberations of this panel.

A group of assessors reviewed and adjudicated the plans at each game turn and also identified issues and insights. Computer models were not used in the adjudication process and the adjudications did not affect the succeeding prepared vignettes.

ATWG 2000 THEMES

In support of the Army's transformation strategy, ATWG 2000 attempted to answer three questions: (1) Why an Army? (2) Why this Army? (3) What are the compelling insights for an Army in 2015? Several focus areas and associated issues were developed prior to the game for each of these themes.[3] The examination of the issues during the game, in the context of the vignettes, was designed to assist analysts in developing insights "into the basis for achieving overmatch against a multi-dimensional threat across the full spectrum of operations" (TRADOC, 2000d).

The following discussions summarize the game events that led to the insight reported in italics below. The insights were developed by RAND analysts while observing game play and participating in the deliberations of the Strategic Insights Panel. The evidence from the game, however, was not always sufficiently compelling to claim the insight is more broadly applicable. Consequently, most insights are stated in terms of the game. More research is needed to assess their wider applicability.

WHY AN ARMY?

ATWG 2000 highlighted some fundamental dimensions of the Army's potential contributions to national security.

---

[3]See Appendix D of TRADOC (2000d) for a complete list of the focus areas and issues.

Controlling Territory

During ATWG 2000, Army forces were essential to accomplish the following missions:

- Defeat and eject NIR forces from Syria and Turkey.

- Restore and ensure territorial integrity of Syria and Turkey.

- Defeat NIR forces in Iraq and seize control of population centers to facilitate splitting the NIR and establishing a separate Iraqi regime.

- Eliminate NIR's capability to conduct aggression.[4]

To accomplish this, *the Army was needed to control large expanses of territory for an extended period of time—a mission the other armed services could not accomplish. Within this mission, the national command authority (NCA) may require the Army to establish conditions favorable for changes to government and society.*

Large-Scale Conventional Combat

ATWG 2000 focused on Army capabilities, while also recognizing the capabilities of other services were essential to campaign success. The wargame highlighted the Army's ability to seize and hold terrain because the mission included expulsion of enemy forces from terrain it had overrun. Game play focused more on the warfighting capabilities of a notional force representing the Objective Force whose composition is yet to be determined; it concentrated less on the broader capabilities of the total Army.

Game players recognized that the Army's capability to conduct stability operations to assist locally in the transition from war to peace would be crucial both during and after combat operations.[5] In this scenario, *large-scale conventional land combat played a central role. Force was required to defeat the enemy's conventional military forces,*

---

[4]Briefing, National Security Seminar, "Blue Operational Team 1, Military Options (CONOPS)," Slide 1 (Restated Mission).

[5]Throughout the conflict, Red attempted to complicate Blue's task by causing as many refugees as possible, thus creating the need for early stability and support operations.

to control critical terrain, and to conduct stability operations. Only the Army could provide these essential capabilities.

Opportunities for Land Power

The Army forces that were played during ATWG 2000 deployed with great rapidity. If the Army could deploy a force on the timelines postulated in this game, the United States could transition to offensive operations much earlier than it currently does. In the vignette presented to Operational Insights Panel 1, the United States rapidly deployed a division-sized task force as a deterrent measure, causing NIR leadership to postpone its planned offensive for approximately one year.

After deterrence failed, the United States and its allies sought to rapidly eject NIR forces from positions it had seized. Moreover, it intended to split the NIR back into the separate countries of Iran and Iraq. To attain these goals, the United States needed powerful land forces, capable of offensive operations against a large, well-armed opponent.

The rapid deployment of a decisive Army force contributed to the temporary deterrence of the NIR and helped terminate the conflict more quickly when deterrence failed.

Restrictions on Land Power

The Objective Force played in the game was designed to conduct vertical envelopment.[6] The feasibility of this concept is sensitive to opposing air defense, especially non-emitting air defenses. Had the NIR fielded a more effective air defense, the United States would either have suffered larger combat losses or consequently been forced to conduct a ground-centric maneuver to achieve its objectives.

Opposing air defenses may restrict the tactic of vertical envelopment.

---

[6]Vertical envelopment is a tactical maneuver in which troops, either air-dropped or air-landed, attack the rear and flanks of a force, in effect cutting off or encircling the force (Joint Publication 1-02).

WHY THIS ARMY?

ATWG 2000 highlighted contributions of the Objective Force, which was designed to conduct vertical envelopment as one of its key attributes.

Rapid Deployment

RAND Insight: More rapid deployment of land power would give the NCA new options, especially during the first phase of a campaign. However, deciding whether to go on the offensive early or to pause while building up combat power would depend on the situation. Sometimes, an early transition to the offensive would be optimal while at other times, a deliberate build-up would be best.

During the Army Transformation process, TRADOC should consider not only the benefits of rapid transition to the offensive, but also cases in which deliberate build-up is more advantageous.

Army Transformation

During the game the Army relied heavily on units that used the Future Transport Rotorcraft (FTR) to lift the Future Combat System (FCS). However, these programs have inherent risks. The FCS may not be sufficiently survivable to employ successfully in combat against an opponent with modern heavy forces. The Army may not be able to fund adequate numbers of the FTR and other services may be unwilling to assist. Additionally, the FTR may not be sufficiently survivable against opposing air defenses.

The Army should consider several operational concepts to hedge against failure in case a concept emphasizing operational maneuver by air proves to be infeasible or unaffordable.

Members of the Strategic Insights Panel believed the Army could not successfully field the Objective Force played in the game through its own unaided efforts. Achieving the capabilities of the Objective Force would require programs across the Department of Defense (DoD), not simply within the Army alone. These programs would include: space assets to support greatly improved reconnaissance and broad bandwidth communications, improved airlift capabilities, means to suppress air defense at low altitude, and new control systems to integrate air and land operations.

Army Transformation demands a joint effort embracing programs conducted by DoD and other services

Jointness

In Vignette 2, one brigade of the 82nd Airborne Division operated with elements of the 3rd Aerospace Expeditionary Force to suppress part of the Red air defense system. Integration of this sort was essential to realize the full combat potential of the Objective Force units.

In the game, maximizing the effectiveness in combat of Objective Force units required an unprecedented degree of integration with air forces.

Situational Awareness

Throughout the game, Blue was assumed to have situational awareness that was vastly superior to Red's, although still imperfect. Certainly, forces conducting vertical envelopment would require excellent situational awareness to operate successfully at low altitudes in the presence of enemy air defense. Even small imperfections—for example, not knowing where small air defense units were located—could have serious consequences.

The Objective Force will not have perfect situational awareness using current or projected systems and procedures, but small imperfections could have serious consequences for forces conducting operational maneuver by air.

During the game, the high-altitude communications nodes were initially assumed to be invulnerable to conventional high-altitude air defense. Despite this, Red Panel 1 employed hypothetical microrockets to attack high-altitude communications nodes within range. These attacks were adjudicated to be successful against nodes in eastern Iraq and the Persian Gulf. Loss of these nodes may have caused loss of high-bandwidth communications for the deployed Objective Force units.

The Objective Force required highly robust communications with high bandwidth to support intertheater combat service support; intelligence, surveillance, and reconnaissance; and the tasking, processing, exploitation, and dissemination of intelligence data.

ACKNOWLEDGMENTS

We thank Margaret Fratzel, TRADOC Analysis Center, Fort Leaven-worth, Kansas, for commenting on a first draft of this document and, in general, for being an ideal colleague. We thank Col. (ret.) Richard (Rick) Hart Sinnreich for his keen observations and insights. We acknowledge the help of Brig. Gen. (ret.) Huba Wass de Czege, whose innovative thinking was central to the Army After Next process and to the Army Transformation Wargame described here.

ACRONYMS

AAN	Army After Next
AAR	After action review
AEF	Aerospace Expeditionary Force
ATO	Air tasking order
ATWG 2000	Army Transformation Wargame 2000
CINC	Commander in Chief
CND	Computer Network Defense
CONOPS	Concept of operations
CRAF	Civil Reserve Air Fleet
CSS	Combat service support
DoD	Department of Defense
FCS	Future Combat System
FTR	Future Transport Rotorcraft
GBL	Ground-based laser
GEO	Geosynchronous earth orbit
HPM	High-power microwave
IBCT	Interim Brigade Combat Team

IO	Information operations
ISR	Intelligence, surveillance, and reconnaissance
I&W	Indications and warning
LEO	Low earth orbit
MANPADS	Man-portable air defense systems
MEO	Medium earth orbit
MTW	Major theater war
NAC	North Atlantic Council
NATO	North Atlantic Treaty Organization
NCA	National Command Authority
NIR	New Independent Republic
SASO	Stability and security operations
SATCOM	Satellite communications
SIP	Strategic Insights Panel
SPOD	Seaport of debarkation
TMD	Theater missile defense
TPED	Tasking, processing, exploitation, and dissemination
TRADOC	U.S. Army Training and Doctrine Command
UAV	Unmanned aerial vehicle
UK	United Kingdom
UN	United Nations
USAF	U.S. Air Force
USMC	U.S. Marine Corps

USN	U.S. Navy
USA	U.S. Army
VISA	Voluntary Intermodal Sealift Agreement

Chapter One

INTRODUCTION

The Chief of Staff of the Army recently announced a strategy to transform the Army over the next two to three decades into a force that will remain dominant across the full spectrum of operations while becoming strategically more responsive. This strategy encompasses a Legacy Force, an Interim Force, and an Objective Force.

THE TRANSFORMATION FORCE

The Legacy Force includes portions of today's Army modernized through existing programs, especially the insertion of information technology. The Interim Force currently comprises two Interim Brigade Combat Teams (IBCTs) forming at Fort Lewis, Washington, using leased vehicles. It will eventually comprise up to eight brigade combat teams (including at least one reserve component team), equipped with an Interim Armored Vehicle, an off-the-shelf, medium-weight vehicle deployable by C-130 aircraft.[1] The Army is also considering formation of Interim Divisions composed of IBCTs and redesigned corps, divisional and Army service component command headquarters, as well as combat support and combat service support units at echelons above division. The Interim Force will respond to the Army's immediate operational requirements and also serve as a "vanguard of the future Objective Force" (Shinseki, 2000a, p. 28). Based on plans to be completed in 2003, the Army will invest in research and development over a period of eight to ten years.

---

[1] The Light Armored Vehicle (LAV III)—manufactured jointly by General Motors Canada and General Dynamics Land Forces Division—has been selected.

When technologies are mature, the Army will start fielding the Objective Force in unit sets called Objective Brigade Combat Teams. It will transform the Legacy Force first and then the Interim Force. The Chief of Staff set ambitious deployment goals for the Objective Force: deployment of a brigade in 96 hours, a division in 120 hours, and five divisions in 30 days. A notional transformation timeline is depicted in Figure 1.1.

THE TRANSFORMATION WARGAME

The Training and Doctrine Command (TRADOC)–sponsored Army Transformation Wargame 2000 (ATWG 2000) was held at the Army War College in Carlisle, Pennsylvania, from April 30 to May 5, 2000. The game had three purposes: (1) to support the Army Transformation to the Objective Force, (2) to provide a visualization of a possible strategic and operational environment for this force, and (3) to facilitate understanding of the Army vision.[2]

RAND *MR1335-F-1.1*

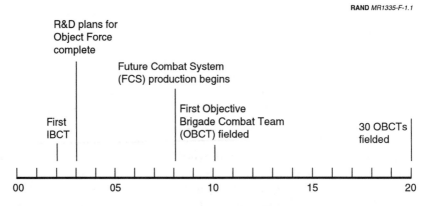

Figure 1.1—Notional Transformation Timeline

---

[2]U.S. Army Training and Doctrine Command (TRADOC), *Army Transformation Wargame 2000, Game Book*, Fort Monroe, Va., 2000d.

SCENARIO

ATWG 2000 was a free-play, two-sided, operational-level, seminar-wargame conducted in three sequential and independent vignettes. The vignettes were independent in that decisions made during the preceding vignette did not affect the situation at the start of the next one. The vignettes covered crisis response, warfighting, and post-conflict operations.

The scenario was set in Southwest Asia in the 2015 time frame. The New Independent Republic (NIR) composed of the former Iraq and Iran threatened Turkey and Syria over water rights to the Tigris and Euphrates rivers. The United States entered the conflict on the side of North Atlantic Treaty Organization (NATO) ally Turkey to defend it and its neighbor, Syria, against a possible invasion by the NIR.

GAME STRUCTURE

The structure of the game is illustrated in Figure 1.2. There were two types of "insights" panels: the Operational Insights Panels focused on the vignettes and the Strategic Insights Panel (SIP) focused on broad issues. The Operational Insights Panels consisted of two Blue-Red pairs and focused on the vignettes. Each of these pairs was presented with different vignettes within the context of the same scenario.

The Operational Insights Panels produced plans (Red and Blue) as a result of the vignettes presented to them and the concept of operations (CONOPS) prepared during the March 2000 Military Planning Seminar.[3] During ATWG 2000, each panel played a two-sided seminar wargame, thus allowing consideration of two different cases.

The SIP had oversight of both cases and consisted of functional area specialists. During each vignette, their mission was to consider a set of issues within the context of the vignettes and to develop issues and insights not directly associated with the vignettes. Team members were free to visit the Operational Insights Panels during their deliberations to gain an understanding of operational issues.

---

[3]The Military Planning Seminar was designed to produce concept plans for both Red and Blue forces. It was held in Washington, D.C., from March 14 to 17, 2000.

RAND *MR1335-F-1.2*

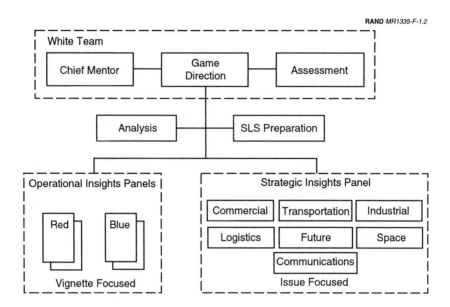

Figure 1.2—ATWG 2000 Game Structure

A group of assessors reviewed and adjudicated the plans at each game turn and also identified issues and insights. Computer models were not used in the adjudication process and the adjudications did not affect the succeeding prepared vignettes.

ATWG 2000 THEMES

In support of the Army's transformation strategy, ATWG 2000 attempted to answer three questions: (1) Why an Army? (2) Why this Army? (3) What are the compelling insights for an Army in 2015? Several focus areas and associated issues were developed prior to the game for each of these themes.[4] During the game, the examination of the issues, in the context of the vignettes, was to provide insights "into the basis for achieving overmatch against a multi-dimensional threat across the full spectrum of operations"(TRADOC, 2000d).

---

[4]TRADOC (2000d), Appendix D: ATWG 2000 Themes, Focus Areas & Issues.

ORGANIZATION OF THIS REPORT

Of the several issues associated with the two themes and their included focus areas, only those that generated interesting insights are addressed in this report. Chapters Two and Three present insights into these issues generated by the RAND analysts observing and participating in the game. These sections follow the format used by the SIP: (1) issues as formulated in the *Game Book*,[5] (2) insights that emerged from game play, and (3) discussion supporting the insights. Chapter Four outlines how the Army might pursue the research goals of the ATWG process. The Appendix describes the design of ATWG 2000.

It is important to note here that the evidence from the game was not always sufficiently compelling to claim that the insights are more broadly applicable. Consequently, most are stated in terms of the game.

---

[5]TRADOC (2000d), Appendix D: ATWG 2000 Themes, Focus Areas & Issues, pp. 59–62.

Chapter Two

WHY AN ARMY?

This section responds to the question "Why an Army?," drawing on the ATWG 2000 for insights.

ATWG 2000 illustrated why the nation will need an Army to achieve the goals established within the scenario played. It did this by highlighting some of the Army's unique contributions toward meeting the campaign objectives posited in the scenario. These include the ability to control large amounts of territory for extended periods of time and to create conditions for desired political change.

What follows is a series of insights associated with the focus area issues (in italics) within the "Why an Army?" theme. RAND analysts observing the game and participating in the SIP developed these insights.

REQUIREMENT FOR AN ARMY: CONTROL OF TERRITORY

What are the conditions and challenges of the 2015 strategic/ operational environment that define the requirement for an Army?

During the game, the Army was needed to control large expanses of territory for several months—a mission the other armed services could not accomplish. Within this mission, the national command authority (NCA) may increasingly require the Army to establish conditions favorable for changes to government and society—a mission that only the Army can accomplish.

During ATWG 2000, Army forces were essential to accomplish the following missions:

- Defeat and eject NIR forces from Syria and Turkey.

- Restore and ensure territorial integrity of Syria and Turkey.

- Defeat NIR forces in Iraq and seize control of population centers to facilitate splitting the NIR and establishing a separate Iraqi regime.

- Eliminate NIR's capability to conduct aggression.[1]

Restore and ensure territorial integrity. The scenario presented to Panel 1 featured a six-corps attack by the NIR into Syria to gain physical control over the Euphrates River. Under cover of repetitive, large-scale exercises, the NIR attacked rapidly on a broad front. After NIR forces attained their objectives in Syria, they quickly transitioned to preplanned defensive "webs," (i.e., autonomous groups of mutually supporting force elements). The Blue President directed a notional Commander in Chief (CINC) west to defeat and eject NIR forces. During the game, II Marine Expeditionary Force deployed into Tripoli and V Corps (1st Infantry Division, 1st Armored Division, 3rd Armored Cavalry Regiment) deployed into Beirut. In addition, V Corps exercised operational control over coalition forces: 1st United Kingdom (UK) Armored Division, 3rd UK Armored Division, and 7th German Mechanized Division. These forces rapidly cleared Syria and advanced to positions north of Baghdad.

The scenario presented to Panel 2 featured an airborne assault by NIR forces to secure the Ataturk Dam at the headwaters of the Euphrates River. The NIR advanced into Turkish territory with its II Corps in an attempt to link with these airborne forces. Blue helped break up this attack through vertical envelopment of the NIR 44th Mechanized Division using two brigades from 101st Air Assault Division (Objective Force).

Establishing a separate Iraqi regime. In both scenarios, the Blue President set the objective of dismembering the NIR (i.e., detaching Iraq from Iran, and establishing an acceptable government in Iraq). At game's end in both panels, Blue Army forces were closing on Baghdad in the culmination of successful campaigns. Panel mem-

---

[1]Briefing, National Security Seminar, "Blue Operational Team 1, Military Options (CONOPS)," Slide 1 (Restated Mission).

bers began planning post-conflict missions, including humanitarian assistance and restoration of civil order. They foresaw that ground forces would be heavily involved with Iraqi society for at least several months until the United Nations (UN) could establish a mission.

Eliminate NIR's capability to conduct aggression. Following establishment of a UN mission in Iraq, panel members foresaw that the U.S. Army would remain deployed in Iraq for years, possibly as long as a decade. The Army would have to secure Iraq's border for several years. It would also need to assist in internal security if Iran sponsored terrorism and guerrilla activity in Iraq. The Army would help equip and train new Iraqi forces while instilling democratic practice.

DEMANDS ON AN ARMY: CENTRAL ROLE OF LAND COMBAT FORCES

Given the conditions and challenges of the future environment, what are the strategic and operational demands on an Army in 2015 concerning engagement, crisis response, warfighting, and post-conflict operations?

In this scenario, large-scale conventional land combat played a central role. Force was required to defeat the enemy's conventional military forces, control critical terrain, and conduct stability operations. Only the Army could provide these essential capabilities.

ATWG 2000 focused on Army capabilities, while also recognizing the capabilities of other services were essential to success. The wargame highlighted the Army's ability to seize and hold terrain because the mission included expulsion of enemy forces from terrain it had overrun. Game play focused more on the warfighting capabilities of a notional force representing the Objective Force whose composition is yet to be determined; it concentrated less on the broader capabilities of the total Army. But game players recognized that the Army's capability to conduct stability operations would be crucial both during and after combat operations.

DIFFERENCES FROM TODAY: INSIGHT OF OPERATIONS IN COMPLEX TERRAIN

How do these demands differ from today?

In the future, the Army will likely face opponents who choose to operate in complex terrain in order to minimize the impact of U.S. superiority in fire and maneuver.

ATWG 2000 extrapolated current trends into the future. It was based on assumptions that projected these trends: The principal actors will continue to be states; the United States will remain strong and globally engaged, the gap between developed and undeveloped states will widen, and non-state actors will increasingly influence world politics. In light of this, an opponent will likely develop concepts to exploit U.S. vulnerabilities; seize important objectives before U.S. forces can deploy; deny entry of U.S. forces; adversely influence U.S. national will by causing mass casualties; preferentially operate in complex terrain; resort to terrorism, etc. Almost certainly, future opponents will employ such concepts. Indeed, Saddam Hussein, despite being a notably inept strategist, attempted most of them during the Gulf War.

In addition to extrapolating present trends into the future without discontinuity, members of the SIP thought the Army may also want to consider discontinuities that would present new challenges. Weapons of mass destruction are an example. During ATWG 2000, the enemy had nuclear weapons, but chose to withhold them as an ultimate guarantee of regime survival. As a result, these weapons sparked a few debates but had little influence on the course of game play. However, weapons of mass destruction might not always remain in friendly hands. They might proliferate into the hands of reckless dictators or even terrorist organizations. How could the Army operate successfully in such an environment while limiting casualties of itself and civilian populations?

Assuming that current trends continue smoothly into the future, opponents will present greater challenges than did the Iraqis during Operation Desert Storm. During ATWG 2000, NIR commanders were highly conscious of U.S. superiority in fire and maneuver. To minimize the effects of this superiority, they preferred to operate in the most difficult terrain, including urban areas.

UNIQUE CAPABILITIES: ADVANTAGES OF RAPID DEPLOYMENT

What are the unique capabilities that an Army provides to the nation in 2015?

The rapid deployment of a decisive Army force contributed to the initial deterrence of the NIR and helped terminate the conflict more quickly when deterrence failed a year later.

The Army forces played during ATWG 2000 deployed with great rapidity. If Army forces could deploy in 2015 on the timelines postulated in this game, the United States could transition to offensive operations much earlier than is currently the case. In Panel 1, the United States rapidly deployed a division-sized task force as a deterrent measure, causing the NIR leadership to postpone its planned offensive for approximately one year.

DECISIVE FORCE: EARLY CONFLICT TERMINATION

What constitutes decisive capabilities and decisive force in 2015?

Decisive operations imply the ability to terminate conflict quickly on terms favorable to attainment of U.S. strategic goals.

After deterrence failed, the United States and its allies sought to rapidly eject NIR forces from positions they had seized in Syria (Panel 1) or Turkey and Syria (Panel 2). Moreover, the United States intended to split the NIR back into the separate countries of Iran and Iraq. To attain these goals it needed powerful land forces, capable of offensive operations against a large, well-armed opponent. By the end of the game, the NIR had suffered considerable losses in its conventional forces and was on the verge of being dissolved politically. It was not clear how long or in what strength the United States and its allies would have to remain in the area to assure that the NIR would not be reconstituted. In addition, most players thought the forces would have to assist in restoring government functions and perhaps in constructing a viable post-conflict government in the former Iraqi territory.

RESTRICTIONS ON LAND POWER: VERTICAL ENVELOPMENT[2]

What conditions restrict the use of land power in 2015, and how can these be mitigated?

Opposing air defenses might restrict the use of vertical envelopment.

ATWG 2000 featured an Objective Force that was designed to conduct vertical envelopment. The feasibility of this concept was sensitive to opposing air defense, especially non-emitting air defenses such as man-portable air defense systems (MANPADS) at low and mid-altitude. Had the NIR fielded a more effective air defense, the United States would either have suffered larger combat losses or else conducted ground-centric maneuver to achieve its objectives. Since the NCA and CINC did not face this problem during the game, their response is a matter for speculation; they likely would have preferred to conduct ground maneuver complemented with vertical insertions outside the range of opposing air defense.

---

[2]Vertical envelopment is a tactical maneuver in which troops, either air-dropped or air-landed, attack the rear and flanks of a force, in effect cutting off or encircling the force (Joint Publication 1-02).

Chapter Three

WHY THIS ARMY?

This chapter responds to the question "Why this Army?," drawing on ATWG 2000 for insights. "This Army" implies the Objective Force, presented in the wargame as forces designed to conduct operational maneuver by air.

As in the previous chapter, a series of insights associated with the focus area issues (in italics) within the theme "Why this Army?" follows. The RAND analysts observing the game and participating in the SIP developed these insights.

EMPLOYMENT OF FORCES: EMPLOYING RAPID DEPLOYMENT

To meet the changing operational environment and mission requirements, what are the changes required in the way we must construct the battle space of the future—the way we plan, coordinate, and employ forces to remain dominant in that environment?

During ATWG 2000, the United States could not deploy land forces rapidly enough to prevent NIR forces from occupying large portions of Syria. Objective Force units initially deployed to forward staging bases—such as Cyprus and Turkey—to deter further aggression and prepare for subsequent operations. Thereafter, time generally worked to the advantage of the United States and its allies. With each passing day, allied strength increased until it became overwhelming. This overpowering force outweighed any improvements NIR forces could make to their defensive positions during the period of allied force build-up. On a greatly compressed timeline, the situation was comparable to the defense phase of the Gulf War. During Operation Desert Shield, the coalition partners took months to build up their forces, confident that this force advantage would far outweigh any improvements Iraqi forces could make to their defensive positions in and around Kuwait.

Members of the SIP believed the United States would require rapidly deploying land forces to deter or defeat certain enemy actions early in a campaign. For example, land forces may be required to evacuate U.S. nationals, rescue hostages, conduct raids against key enemy capabilities, reassure allies, deter further aggression, and secure key terrain. Some of these missions would require small forces, such as special operations forces, Marine Expeditionary Units, and battalion-sized Army formations. Other missions would require larger forces, including brigade- and division-sized Army formations. Later in the campaign, the United States may elect to pause in air-land operations and exploit its superiority in air and at sea to conduct a deliberate build-up of forces until it achieved overwhelming superiority.

RAND Insight: During the initial phase of a campaign, there can be a window of opportunity when rapid deployment is needed to avoid unacceptable strategic gains by the adversary. After this window closes, the United States may elect to pause in air-land operations while building up overwhelming force.

FORCE DESIGN: ALTERNATIVE FORCE DESIGNS

What are the implications of a full-spectrum force design?

"Full spectrum" implies conducting different types of operations to accomplish missions during peacetime engagement, smaller-scale contingencies, and major theater war (MTW). A full-spectrum design would ensure that the Army is prepared to conduct such a range of operations simultaneously or sequentially.

During ATWG 2000, the Army relied heavily on forces that used the Future Transport Rotorcraft (FTR) to lift the Future Combat System (FCS). But these programs have inherent risks. The FCS may not be sufficiently armored to employ successfully in combat at the upper end of the spectrum against an opponent with modern heavy forces.

Additionally, the FTR may not be sufficiently survivable against opposing air defenses.

A 20-ton FCS would not offer passive protection against large anti-tank missiles and long-rod penetrators. It may be possible to develop an effective system of active protection against relatively slow-moving anti-tank missiles, but there is little midterm prospect of defeating the long-rod penetrator. FCS could be made more survivable in other ways such as improving situational awareness and robotics—for example, using an unmanned variant for armed reconnaissance. If at the time of a procurement decision, FCS lacks survivability against an opponent with modern heavy forces, it would not be employable across the full spectrum.

ENSURING OVERMATCH: JOINT DEVELOPMENT OF ARMY TRANSFORMATION FORCE

What are the critical areas for ensuring overmatch in the Objective Force design in 2015?

Army Transformation demands a joint effort embracing programs conducted by other services and the Department of Defense (DoD).

Members of the SIP thought that the Army could not successfully field the Objective Force played in ATWG 2000 through its own unaided efforts. To achieve overmatch of the Objective Force would require programs across DoD not simply within the Army alone. These programs would include: space assets to support greatly improved reconnaissance and broad bandwidth communications, improved airlift capabilities, means to suppress air defense at low altitude, and new control systems to integrate air and land operations.

CRISIS RESPONSE: RAPID RESPONSE

How does this Army expand NCA options for crisis response?

In the game, the medium-weight Objective Force was more rapidly deployable than current Army forces. This gave the NCA a new option to deter the NIR and reassure the allies by moving quickly to insert forces into the theater.

In Panel 1, rapid deployment of U.S. forces initially deterred Red, which waited a year before attacking. The ATWG 2000 scenario allowed the United States to execute Flexible Deterrent Options well in advance of hostilities. The Panel 1 Blue commander thought his optimal strategy was to deliberately build up forces before initiating an air-land campaign, while expanding and exploiting his superiority in air and at sea. The corresponding Red commander subsequently stated that "in [Red] Team 1. . .offensive planning was utterly unaffected by the threat of Blue ground force deployments of less than corps size whatever their speed of arrival."[1]

RAND Insight: The Red forces played in ATWG 2000 were so large that deploying a brigade in 96 hours had little impact on events. The most relevant deployment goal was five divisions in 30 days, a force sufficiently large to have operational impact.

In both panels, Blue could not prevent Red from invading Syria and Turkey, but Red did not achieve any decisive advantage through these invasions. Even if Red had completely occupied Syria, Blue would still have maintained ports of entry in Lebanon and would have been under no great pressure to expel Red quickly. Blue players recognized that U.S. public opinion would demand that NATO allies assume a fair share of the burdens and risks of a campaign. U.S. domestic support would decline quickly if it appeared that the United States was assuming a disproportionate share. For this reason, Blue could not initiate operations in advance before the NATO allies were ready and therefore was constrained by their deployment time, regardless of how fast U.S. forces deployed.

DEPLOYMENT GOALS

What changes within and outside the Army will be required in the next 15 years to accomplish the Army's deployment goals?

---

[1]Personal communication between the authors and the Red Team 1 commander.

Lift Assets

The Army will have to compete for airlift and make a persuasive case for early-arriving Army forces. In addition, considerable increases in fast sealift and prepositioning would be required.

The Army could sponsor development and procurement of aircraft dedicated to lifting land forces. One such possibility is the FTR. (FTR is a joint program in conceptual phase with Army lead, which may develop either a tilt-rotor or rotary-wing aircraft.) ATWG 2000 played 512 FTRs, used primarily by the 82nd Airborne Division and 101st Air Assault Division. However, to employ 512 aircraft in the area of operations, the total buy would probably exceed 600 aircraft including the training base and maintenance reserve. The Army may not be able to afford such a large buy. Historically, the Army has been a user of airlift procured almost entirely by the Air Force. It is not clear if the Air Force would purchase large numbers of FTRs; if it did they would presumably support the combatant command and might or might not be allocated exclusively to Army units.

Considerable technical and programmatic reasons issues will have to be resolved to successfully field the FTR in the numbers required. Historically, major aircraft programs have lengthy timelines. For example, development of the RAH-66 Comanche helicopter began in 1984. The program received approval to enter engineering and manufacturing development in April 2000 and according to current plans, the first operational unit will be formed at the end of 2006— over two decades after the program began. Development of the V-22 Osprey tilt-rotor aircraft took roughly 15 years to the time of initial production; fielding the aircraft will probably be a lengthy process. DoD usually authorizes low-rate initial production of a new aircraft for several years before going to full-scale production. Given the likely cost of the FTR, production rates would probably be in the range of 20 to 40 aircraft per year. Based on past experience, fielding a large fleet of FTRs would be a very difficult task.

The Army typically gets less than one-half of airlift during the initial two to three weeks of build-up phase for an MTW.[2] During this

---

[2]In August 1990, the Army received 47 percent of the passenger lift and 46 percent of the Desert Shield cargo airlift. See Matthews (1996), p 41.

period, it typically receives airlift to deploy certain critical assets (such as light forces) and Patriot batteries, but seldom to lift heavy maneuver forces. To receive a larger allocation, the Army would have to compete successfully against other high priority items such as logistic support for Aerospace Expeditionary Forces (AEFs), which might already be engaged in combat operations. To make a persuasive case, the Army component would have to convince the combatant commander that early arrival of maneuver forces would confer important advantages. He might, for example, argue that early-arriving maneuver forces would confront an enemy with a dilemma: disperse to hide from air forces or concentrate to oppose land forces.

Improved Indications and Warning

To deter opposing action prior to hostilities, the United States requires extremely reliable indications and warning (I&W).

To support the high-level decision to commit U.S. forces during the game, it was assumed that extremely reliable I&W was available. Such I&W would probably require a wide range of collection, including human intelligence as well as collection through space-based and theater assets. Even so, the process might eventually founder on the traditional controversy over capabilities and intent. For example, up to a few days prior to the onset of hostilities, Saddam Hussein was assessed as having the capability to occupy Kuwait, but not the intent.[3]

Early NCA Deployment Decision

To achieve the advantages of rapid deployment requires early deployment decisions from the NCA, earlier than in the past.

During ATWG 2000, the U.S. NCA declared C-Day, activated Civil Reserve Air Fleet (CRAF) II, invoked the Voluntary Intermodal Sealift

---

[3]On July 31, the Commander in Chief, U.S. Central Command, General H. Norman Schwarzkopf assessed that hostilities were imminent, but believed the Iraqis would seize only the Rumaila oil field and Bubiyan Island, not the entire country. Saddam attacked on the second day of August and overran Kuwait in three days (Schwarzkopf, 1992, pp. 294–295).

Agreement (VISA), and ordered a reserve call-up prior to the occurrence of any actual hostility. Indeed, it seems unlikely that any U.S. president would take all these actions in advance of hostilities, even in the face of unambiguous warning. There are precedents for partial call-ups in peacetime, but the full 200,000-man call-up would be very disruptive. The United States has not activated CRAF prior to hostilities and VISA has never been invoked.

SUSTAINMENT

What changes in sustainment will be required to support a strategically responsive full-spectrum Army?

Larger PGM Stocks

All services would require larger stocks of precision-guided munitions to support protracted theater operations by more agile Army forces.

During operations by both Blue panels, the Air Force supported several weeks of high-intensity combat of Army and Marine Corps forces. In Blue Panel 1, for example, the Air Force eventually deployed five AEFs. These forces conducted several large-scale operations to defeat NIR forces in Syria, Kuwait, and Iraq. Air support on this scale was critical, especially during deep vertical envelopment, such as that conducted in central Iraq by elements of the 82nd Airborne Division. But providing air support on this scale would have quickly consumed large stocks of precision-guided munitions, more than the Air Force is planning to buy during the scenario's time frame. Without precision-guided munitions, air operations would be considerably less effective, possibly jeopardizing success of operations by the highly agile Objective Force.

Aerial Resupply

The Objective Force maneuvered over very large operational areas at extended distances from bases. Support for these operations would likely require combat service support (CSS) units capable of aerial resupply and aerial medical evacuation with treatment enroute.

The Blue panels planned to insert two Objective Force units deep into the enemy rear to isolate and destroy NIR units. No landlines of communications were established and the distances were beyond the range of existing rotary-wing aircraft. To support this maneuver, either the CSS units would have to be equipped with FTRs or the combatant commander would have to allocate large numbers of C-130 sorties to sustain the Objective Force units. If C-130s were used, the Objective Force units would be tethered to landing fields. In either case, the combatant command would need to establish secure air corridors.

Medical support would be of particular concern during such deep operations. During ATWG 2000, Objective Force units suffered significant numbers of casualties in the early war stages. They sustained these casualties prior to establishment of a theater medical or evacuation infrastructure, significantly increasing the risk of deaths occurring before arrival at definitive care facilities. In view of the lengthy evacuation times, Objective Force units would require better means of stabilizing patients than are currently available.

Commercial Logistic Support

Very rapid deployment may imply changes to current procedures for commercial contracting of logistic support.

Members of the SIP noted that in recent years, the Army has depended increasingly on commercial contracting to support its deployed forces. These contracts have provided high-quality support, usually at significantly less cost (especially in manpower) than the Army would incur by using its own resources. However, very rapid deployment will require significant changes in the procedures for contracting commercial support to assure its timeliness.

OBJECTIVE FORCE CHARACTERISTICS: RISKS OF VERTICAL ENVELOPMENT

How do the Objective Force characteristics enable it to meet the operational demands of 2015?

To be fully effective at acceptable risk, vertical envelopment may require suppression of low-altitude air defense.

Members of the SIP noted the Objective Force played in ATWG 2000 might be at risk to opposing air defense. To conduct vertical envelopment in the presence of opposing forces, lifters would often have to fly within range of air defenses, especially air defenses at low altitude—that is, less than 15,000 feet above ground level. At low altitude, opposing forces could employ missiles with passive guidance, anti-aircraft guns, general-purpose machine guns, anti-helicopter mines, and small arms. In recent air operations against Iraq and Yugoslavia, the Air Force, Navy, and Marine Corps aircraft have usually flown at medium altitude to evade low-altitude air defense.

Addressing the low-altitude threat requires detection of the opposing weapons and their suppression. Most of the low-altitude air defense weapons, including MANPADS and anti-aircraft guns do not emit and have minimal signatures. As a result, they are difficult to detect and usually even survive an extended air campaign. Under strict rules of engagement, air defense suppression may also be constrained by risk of collateral damage, as it was during Operation Allied Force.

OBJECTIVE FORCE CAPABILITIES

How do the Objective Force capabilities provide a decisive capability to the Joint Force in 2015?

Situational Awareness

The Objective Force is not likely to attain perfect situational awareness using current or projected systems and procedures, especially during the opening phases of a conflict.

Throughout ATWG 2000, Blue was assumed to have situational awareness that was vastly superior to Red's, if not quite "perfect." Forces conducting operational maneuver by air require excellent situational awareness to operate successfully at low altitude in the presence of enemy air defense. But the Blue panels' assumption that they enjoyed "perfect situational awareness" may not be attainable in the foreseeable future, especially during the first phases of a campaign. Current surveillance and reconnaissance do not nearly provide this level of awareness. The problem areas include detection, geolocation, and timeliness of transmission.

Sufficient Survivable Communications

The Objective Force will require highly robust communications with high bandwidth.

In ATWG 2000, the high-altitude communications nodes were initially assumed to be invulnerable to conventional high-altitude air defense. However, this assumption may not hold. Even high-altitude unmanned aerial vehicles (UAVs) may become vulnerable to advanced surface-to-air missile systems, which may become available to potential adversaries within the next 20 years.

Despite the initial assumption of invulnerability, Red Panel 1 employed microrockets on D+48 to attack high-altitude communications nodes within range. These attacks were adjudicated to be successful against the nodes in eastern Iraq and the Persian Gulf. Loss of these nodes may have caused loss of high bandwidth communications for the deployed Objective Force units.

During subsequent play, it was further assumed that the Objective Force would have a multitiered, redundant communications architecture. This architecture had three layers: high-altitude communications nodes, low earth orbit (LEO) satellite communications (SATCOM), and geosynchronous earth orbit (GEO) SATCOM. Therefore, Objective Force units could switch to LEO SATCOM and GEO SATCOM after high-altitude communications nodes were lost. Current military SATCOM programs will provide insufficient assets to meet the Army's anticipated needs. Commercial SATCOM could provide high-bandwidth communications, given sufficient time and the necessary leasing arrangements. However, it may not be able to provide enough capacity quickly enough unless prior arrangements were made.

Large amounts of high-bandwidth communications will be needed to support intertheater CSS; intelligence, surveillance, and reconnaissance (ISR); and the tasking, processing, exploitation, and dissemination (TPED) of intelligence data.

The Objective Force concept envisions a lean, forward-deployed, CSS, ISR, and TPED structure with focused, just-in-time logistics; a minimal in theater footprint; and nearly perfect situational awareness. To attain these capabilities, the Objective Force will need to "reach back" for necessary support. As noted during ATWG 2000, this concept will require enormous bandwidth. The Army should devise ways to secure the needed bandwidth through both commercial and military assets. In addition, the Objective Force will require communications equipment that supports the required bandwidth, yet is light, small, and reliable.

Lighter-than-air, unmanned, high-altitude communication nodes appear to have significant disadvantages. They require substantial airlift to deploy and may take considerable time for inflation and ascent.

The communication nodes played in ATWG 2000 used a dirigible airframe. They were deployed in compacted form and inflated in theater. Inflation requires large amounts of helium and inflation kits, imposing substantial airlift requirements. Moreover, it can take considerable time to raise these nodes safely to the required altitudes and locations without exposing them to enemy air defenses. Because of these disadvantages, the Army should examine alternatives, especially space-based systems that are linked to highly mobile ground terminals. Selection of a space-based alternative to these nodes would have major implications for space architecture.

Computer Network Defense

The Objective Force may require organic computer network defense (CND) to secure transportation management systems and other critical infrastructure against cyberattacks.

Red Panel 2 used its forces to attack the Blue AEF at the Cairo West Air Base with considerable success using tactical ballistic missiles and information operations (IO). Red may also have launched effective cyberattacks against ports of embarkation and debarkation used by the Objective Force. A sophisticated adversary may be able to disrupt flow through commercial facilities, even to the point of temporarily denying their use. In theater, Objective Force units should employ any organic CND to shield themselves from cyberattacks.

Even in the distant future, there will seldom be enough ISR assets to satisfy the demands of DoD, other U.S. government agencies, and combatant commanders, especially during crisis. To address this problem, TRADOC should consider including tasking requests in future games to estimate the totality of demand and identify the issues associated with allocation of assets. Objective Force units operating at high tempo on a nonlinear battlefield will have especially high demands for ISR. To some extent, they will be able to satisfy these demands using organic assets, but they will also have to draw upon theater assets such as Global Hawk and national assets in space. They will also require extremely rapid TPED of information to operate effectively over long distances at high speed.

Clear Information Operations Policy

The U.S. government needs to develop clear policy guidance and strategy concerning space control and IO.

Space and IO overlap considerably. The United States needs consistent policy across both domains to make the most effective use of its capabilities. In the context of Vignette 1, the Blue NCA established policy that precluded use of Blue capability to control space. Instead, Blue tried to discourage foreign owners of space systems from selling imagery or communications bandwidth to Red. In addition, the United States implemented shutter control mechanisms to prevent Red from using U.S. commercial space assets. The Blue NCA approved early initiation of IO against Red, but not against Red space systems or space-to-ground links. IO could have helped mask the movements of Blue forces and targeting data to Red. They were conducted later in Vignette 2 with considerable success.

IO and Space Control

IO capabilities may prove effective in contributing to a space control strategy.

Blue conducted IO against Red space capabilities only by disabling the ground terminals. It used computer network attacks to cause computer crashes and software corruption or erasure at these sites, causing them to be inoperative for several days. Blue could also have used spoofing to corrupt imagery obtained by Red. This type of IO would be more difficult to detect and therefore could be effective longer than the destructive IO Blue elected to conduct during ATWG 2000.

Integration with Air Forces

In the game, maximizing the effectiveness in combat of Objective Force units required an unprecedented degree of integration with the air forces of other services.

In Vignette 2, one brigade of the 82nd Airborne Division operated with elements of the 3rd AEF to suppress part of the Red air defense system. Integration of this sort was essential to realize the full combat potential of the Objective Force units. However, game players did not consider how this integration could be achieved. Several questions remained unanswered by the players. How might fires of the Army forces and an AEF be integrated most effectively in near–real time? Should the operation have a single commander? If so, how should he be selected? If he were the commander of Army forces, how could his headquarters control air forces effectively from the field? What exercise activity—at the National Training Center or Nellis Air Force Base, for example—would be required to fully develop a concept for integration and assure its smooth execution?

Target Discrimination

Objective Force units will need the ability to distinguish between real and false targets.

During ATWG 2000, Red attempted to overload Blue ISR and TPED using decoys and jamming. For example, it used decoys to simulate transporter-erector-launchers. Red employed this technique in order to overload Blue ISR. In the words of the Red Panel 2 commander: "Total visibility is not perfect situational awareness." Unable to hide from its opponent, Red purposefully presented many false targets. This technique would be affective against current U.S. systems, but hyperspectral sensor imagery systems will soon be available that will allow the United States to distinguish most decoys from real targets.

Limits on Weapons Use

New weapons may have highly important implications for collateral damage.

During ATWG 2000, Blue used high-power microwave (HPM) from a UAV to disrupt NIR forces in Baghdad in support of Task Force Checkmate, although the NIR had declared the Iraqi capital to be an open city. HPM would certainly have damaged civilian infrastructure in the city. Such use may be construed as violating international law and could cause adverse public opinion. The U.S. government needs to develop clear and comprehensive policy on the use of such weapons.

JOINT VISION 2010

What changes in the Army are required to improve integration and achieve the goals of Joint Vision 2010?

Creation of Efficient Processes and Seams

Rather than pursue "seamlessness," the Army should strive to make the "seams" transparent and efficient.

Members of the SIP thought that seamlessness may not always be an achievable or even a desirable goal. For example, the loadmaster on a transport aircraft will normally be a noncommissioned officer in the Air Force, while the Army will often be responsible for loading the aircraft. The interface of these two functions—loading control and loading itself—is a seam. There would be no point in trying to eliminate this seam and therefore seamlessness would be a false goal. The Army and Air Force have a common interest in assuring that aircraft are loaded quickly, efficiently, and safely. The Air Force should clearly promulgate which requirements its loadmasters will enforce. The Army should train its personnel in these requirements and have appropriate material-handling equipment on hand. The complementary functions should be transparent across both services, but the seam between Air Force and Army will remain.

Improved Protection of Debarkation Points

Defense of aerial ports of debarkation and seaports of debarkation (SPODs) against cruise missile attacks demands early employment of theater missile defense (TMD).

In Vignette 1, Blue moved Objective Force units into a Syrian port with a large civilian population. The force was to occupy the port to support future operations. Through sympathizers, the enemy gained targeting data for cruise missile and chemical attacks against this port. Fortunately, Blue had arranged for early deployment of TMD. To ease the pressure on airlift early in a campaign, the United States could provide TMD of SPODs using naval ships.

Enablers for Force Interdependence

To employ the Objective Force effectively, air and land operations must be integrated more closely than they are now.

Members of the SIP discussed the need for greater integration of air and land operations. To open and maintain air corridors for deployment and sustainment of Objective Force units' ground operations, air and land operations would have to be closely synchronized. Air corridors in the area of operations would have to be opened and closed dynamically and monitored carefully to ensure the enemy did not exploit them. Fratricide would be a constant concern in this operational environment. In addition, the air tasking order (ATO) and land force planning cycles would have to be closely synchronized because of the large number of air assets required to support land operations—for example, surveillance platforms, tankers, airlifters, and aircraft specialized in suppression of enemy air defense. The associated issues for control of forces should be explored in future iterations of the ATWG.

TITLE X REQUIREMENTS: STABILITY AND SECURITY OPERATIONS

How does this Army meet Title X requirements of 2015?

The Army may need additional force structure to conduct stability and security operations (SASO) after an MTW.

To conduct SASO in post-conflict Iraq, Blue might have required a variety of units that are not available in sufficient numbers in the current Army force structure. These could include military police units to assure public order, engineer units to restore infrastructure, and medical units to prevent the outbreak of infectious disease. ATWG 2000 terminated just as the full scope of these requirements became apparent to Blue players.

COALITION OPERATIONS: CONSTRAINTS ON FORCE EMPLOYMENT

What are the implications of the Objective Force on the Army's ability to participate in coalition/multinational operations?

The time and effort required to build a coalition might constrain employment of U.S. forces, especially during the early phase of a campaign.

ATWG 2000 obscured the usual difficulties of coalition warfare by giving Blue commanders almost perfect control over allied forces. During Vignette 1, several Blue players in Panel 1 observed that they were functioning as a U.S. command, although the scenario involved NATO countries. At the time when Blue players discussed this issue, they did not know whether Article V of the NATO treaty would be invoked in defense of Turkey. Article V was not invoked, but several NATO countries formed a coalition against the NIR. Germany and the United Kingdom immediately gave operational control of their forces deployed in Syria to the U.S. commander. In a real-world situation, would NATO have operated as an alliance, or would certain NATO countries have formed a coalition of the willing? What command relationships would have emerged in each case? What would be the implications for planning and execution of military operations in each case? If, for example, the overall commander were a NATO commander, what issues would be referred to the North Atlantic Council (NAC) for decision? Would the NAC have approved aggressive use of early-arriving forces? How quickly and completely would individual NATO countries be likely to give operational control of their forces to U.S. commanders? What requirements for consultation might these countries set? Future iterations of the ATWG might be designed to address these issues of coalition war.

ACTIVE/RESERVE COMPONENT INTEGRATION: RESERVE COMPONENT READINESS

What changes in law and policy are necessary to enable the full integration of Active and Reserve components by 2015?

To keep pace with the Objective Force, National Guard units must be more readily deployable than they currently are.

Active Component and Reserve Component integration is likely to become an increasingly important issue in coming years. ATWG 2000 postulated that in 2015, National Guard divisions would be ready for deployment after 75 days of mobilization and training. That level of readiness would be a considerable improvement from today, roughly halving current assumptions. A fundamental objective of the Army vision is to deploy powerful land forces more rapidly in order to achieve quick conflict termination. But accelerated deployment of active units will require the reserve component—especially the National Guard—to increase its readiness posture.

TECHNOLOGY ENABLERS

What technologies/systems provide a significant increase in strategic responsiveness or achievement of full-spectrum dominance?

Ground-Based Lasers

Nondestructive ground-based lasers (GBLs) might deny targeting data to the enemy and delay or prevent attacks on U.S. space assets.

During ATWG 2000, Blue possessed GBLs that could have dazzled opposing sensors, but did not employ them. Blue did try to use diplomacy and shutter control measures to deny Red access to U.S. and third-party commercial imaging satellites. GBLs deploying with the Objective Force could be a better way of denying Red access to surveillance from space. Red may ascribe the results of dazzling to technical difficulties. Moreover, dazzling might be sufficiently discreet enough to inhibit escalation of war into space. However, it is uncertain whether GBLs could be made sufficiently portable to accompany units deployed into a theater of operations. When Red was denied access to space, it tried to "level the playing field" by attacking U.S. space assets.

Satellite Survivability

National and commercial medium earth orbit (MEO) and GEO space systems may be more survivable against future anti-satellite threats than LEO systems.

The Blue forces had a Discoverer II–like system in LEO during ATWG 2000. These systems were vulnerable to Red attacks, but Blue retained other systems in MEO and GEO. These systems helped provide situational awareness to the NCA and combatant commanders. Commercial satellites in LEO were also degraded, but those in GEO were not vulnerable to Red attacks. These results indicate that the Army should promote development and deployment of national assets in MEO and GEO to reduce vulnerability to opposing attacks.

Chapter Four

EXAMINING THE ARMY VISION

This chapter outlines an approach that would help TRADOC to support Army transformation in a systematic way. Similar recommendations were foreshadowed in RAND's report on the 1997 Army After Next (AAN) wargame (Perry and Millot, 1998) and appear in its 1998 Army Technology Seminar Wargame report (Darilek et al., 2001). This approach would link TRADOC-sponsored activities hierarchically in a three-step process.

The first step is to clearly articulate the long-term objectives of the ATWG process. Part of this process is to clearly articulate the goals for the Objective Force: what it is to accomplish, its role in joint and combined operations, and its varied role throughout the spectrum of conflict. A clear statement of these objectives and an understanding of the role of the ATWG process in achieving them is central to a systematic examination of the Army vision.[1]

The second step would be to conduct seminars that bring together military operators and technologists to devise proposed military systems, defined as major end-items of military equipment such as combat vehicles and C4[command, control, communications, and computers]ISR systems. The military operators would articulate desired characteristics and envision how systems might help accomplish missions under varying conditions. The technologists,

---

[1]Focusing on the objectives identifies the values that are of concern to the Army. This is referred to as "value-focused" decisionmaking as opposed to "alternatives-focused" decisionmaking. The former places the process of articulating values over identifying alternatives. Value-focused decisionmaking is discussed in Keeney (1993), pp. 62–67.

including engineers and scientists, would outline relevant technologies and suggest how they might be embodied in militarily useful systems. The output of these seminars would be candidate military systems, based on current or emerging technologies. In the case of emerging technologies, the technologists might also make a first-order assessment of technical risk in developing the systems. The Integrated Idea Teams established by TRADOC are well-suited to accomplish this step.

The third step would be to conduct seminars that draw military experts together to devise notional forces employing the candidate systems. These experts may include company-grade officers with recent tactical experience, field grade officers with broader understanding of military affairs, retired officers with experience at all levels of command, and civilian analysts and theorists. The experts would envision operational concepts to employ the candidate systems in combat, then outline notional forces that would realize the concepts. For example, sudden vertical insertion and fire ambush with long-range precision fires are operational concepts that would help devise notional forces. The output of these seminars would be candidate forces in sufficient detail to permit wargaming. TRADOC has accomplished this step primarily using internal resources. In the future, it might also draw on external resources, for example retired general officers ("graybeards"), industry representatives, and consultants.

The fourth step would be to assemble a wide range of experienced military and civilian personnel for wargames and seminars designed to assess the value of candidate forces in accomplishing missions. Inputs would be the candidate forces and scenarios designed to test utility. The output would be an assessment of the various forces achieved through adjudication, commentary by participants, and subsequent analysis of both sources. A single iteration might be designed to assess just one candidate or several candidates in the same scenario. Figure 4.1 summarizes this recommended approach.

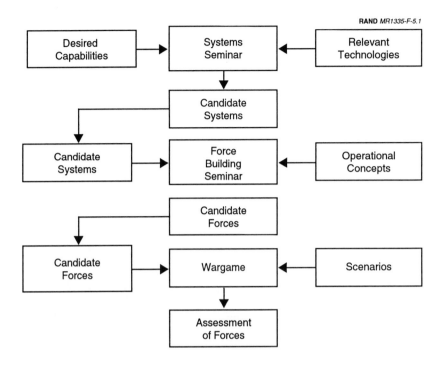

Figure 4.1—Recommended Approach

GAME DESIGN

This Appendix describes the Army Transformation Wargame (ATWG) 2000 game design.

ORGANIZATION OF ATWG 2000

ATWG 2000 included a White team to exercise control, opposed Blue and Red Operational Insights Panels, and a Strategic Insights Panel (SIP). It was conducted in three moves, called "vignettes," designed to explore three phases in a full campaign.

White Team

The White Team included a Chief Mentor, Game Direction, Assessment (Assessment Team 1 and Assessment Team 2), and an Analysis Team. The Chief Mentor developed insights for the Game Director, based on observation of the Operational Insights Panels. Game Direction was responsible for overall conduct of the game. Assessment adjudicated outcomes of opposing plans and identified key insights. The Training and Doctrine Command's Analysis Center led the Analysis Team with support from RAND.

Operational Insights Panels

The Blue and Red teams (officially termed Operational Insights Panels) worked in opposed pairs: Blue 1 opposed Red 1 and Blue 2 opposed Red 2. In this manner, ATWG 2000 allowed consideration of two different cases. The primary function of these panels was to identify and explore insights that evolved during their discussions. Each Blue panel included Senior Mentors, experts replicating the functions of a unified command, and coalition members. Each panel developed a plan for each vignette as in a traditional wargame. In addition, panel members were challenged to develop insights into the Army's issues of concern.

Strategic Insights Panel

An SIP considered both cases developed by the Operational Insights Panels. It was composed of senior individuals with expertise in various functional areas who identified high-level issues and developed insights. Panel members met in committee and at various times observed the Operational Insights Panels and the Assessment Team. In addition, they contributed to the after action review (AAR) process by offering comments on strategic issues. Three RAND analysts were members of the SIP.

Sequence of Events

ATWG 2000 was conducted in three moves, each centering on a vignette. The three vignettes covered crisis response, warfighting, and post-conflict operations. In each move, the Operational Insights Panels were presented a situation and challenged to prepare a response in the form of a conceptual plan to conduct theater-level military operations. In addition, the panels identified key insights. At the end of each move, each opposing pair (Blue 1/Red 1 and Blue 2/Red 2) conducted an AAR under direction of the Chief Mentor and with input from the SIP. During an AAR, each panel presented its plan and raised the issues it considered important. When AARs were conducted, the players did not know how their competing plans would be assessed. Assessment did not affect vignettes, e.g., assessment in Vignette 1 had no impact on the situation described in Vignette 2. However, each vignette built on the preceding vignette, e.g., the situation described in Vignette 2 continued the story begun in Vignette 1 with no consideration given to player decisions.

ATWG GAME PROCESS

The ATWG 2000 followed the process depicted in Figure A.1. The players developed plans based on the situations presented to them and the forces at their disposal. There were no independent functional area advisors. Instead, the Operational Insights Panels included subject area experts to advise panel leaders. The players discussed their plans and perceptions of their opponents' intentions during AARs after each game turn. The SIP observed game play and the assessment process, identified issues, and developed insights. The crucial concern was lack of a feedback loop. Assessment at the end of each vignette did not affect the next vignette. On the contrary, each game move began with a fresh vignette with new start conditions unrelated to game play during the previous vignette. Assessment produced daily outputs as during the AAN games, but they no longer affected play.

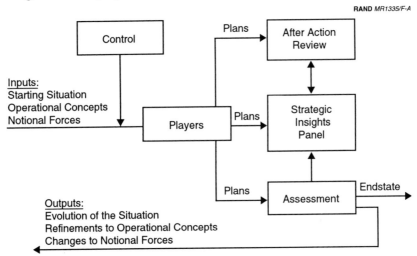

Figure A.1—Structure of Army Transformation Wargame 2000

BIBLIOGRAPHY

Barnett, Jeffrey R., "Funding Two Armies," *Armed Forces Journal International*, May 2000, pp. 14–15.

Darilek, R., et al., *Issues and Insights from the Army Technology Seminar Game*, Santa Monica, Calif.: RAND MR-1299-A, 2001.

Fogleman, Ronald R., General (USAF), and Sheila E. Widnall, Secretary of the Air Force, "Global Engagement: A Vision of the 21st Century Air Force," Headquarters, U.S. Air Force, XPX, Pentagon, Washington, D.C.

Keeney, R. L., "Creativity in MS/OR: Value-Focused Thinking— Creativity Directed Toward Decision Making," *Interfaces*, Vol. 23, No. 3, May–June 1993, pp. 62–67.

Kelso, Frank B., Admiral (USN), and Carl E. Mundy, Jr., General (USMC), "From the Sea, Preparing the Naval Service for the 21st Century," Navy Public Affairs Library, Pentagon, Washington, D.C., 1992, http://www.chinfo.navy.mil/navpalib/policy/fromsea.

Matthews, James K., *So Many, So Much, So Far, So Fast: U.S. Transportation Command and Strategic Deployment for Operation Desert Shield/Desert Storm*. United States Government Printing Office, 1996, p. 41.

Perry, Walter L., and Marc Dean Millot, *Issues from the 1997 Army After Next Winter Wargame*, Santa Monica, Calif.: RAND, MR-998-A, 1998.

Perry, Walter L., Bruce R. Pirnie, and John Gordon IV, *Issues Raised During the Army After Next Spring Wargame*, Santa Monica, Calif.: RAND, MR-1023-A, 1999.

Schwarzkopf, H. Norman, *It Doesn't Take a Hero*, New York: Bantam Books, 1992.

Shalikashvili, John M., General (USA), "Joint Vision 2010," Chairman of the Joint Chiefs of Staff, Pentagon, Washington, D.C., 1999.

Sherman, Jason, "Dream Work," *Armed Forces Journal International*, May 2000, pp. 25–28.

Shinseki, Eric K., General (USA), "The Army Transformation: A Historic Opportunity," *Army*, Vol. 50, No. 10, October 2000a, pp. 21–30.

_____, Chief of Staff, U.S. Army, Statement on the Army Transformation, Airland Subcommittee on Armed Services, U.S. Senate, Second Session, 106th Congress, March 8, 2000b.

TRADOC—*See* U.S. Army Training and Doctrine Command.

U.S. Army, "Army Vision 2010," Headquarters, U.S. Army, Pentagon, Washington, D.C., 2000, http://www.army.mil/2010.

U.S. Army Training and Doctrine Command, *Force XXI Operations: A Concept for the Evolution of Full-Dimensional Operations for the Strategic Army of the Early Twenty-First Century*, TRADOC Pamphlet 525-5, Fort Monroe, Va., 1994.

_____, *Blue Operational Team 1 CONOPS/Plan, U.S. Army Transformation Wargame 2000*, Fort Monroe, Va., 2000a.

_____, *Blue Operational Team 2 CONOPS/Plan, U.S. Army Transformation Wargame 2000*, Fort Monroe, Va., 2000b.

_____, *Future Operational and Threat Environment: A View of the World in 2015, U.S. Army Transformation Wargame 2000*, Fort Monroe, Va., 2000c.

_____, *Game Book, U.S. Army Transformation Wargame 2000*, Fort Monroe, Va., 2000d.

_____, *Military Forces, U.S. Army Transformation Wargame 2000*, Fort Monroe, Va., 2000e.

_____, *Red Operational Team 1 CONOPS/Plan, U.S. Army Transformation Wargame 2000*, Fort Monroe, Va., 2000f.

_____, *Red Operational Team 2 CONOPS/Plan, U.S. Army Transformation Wargame 2000*, Fort Monroe, Va., 2000g.

_____, *White Team Book, U.S. Army Transformation Wargame 2000*, Fort Monroe, Va., 2000h.

Whiteside, Daniel L., Colonel (USA, ret.), "Slow Down!" *Armed Forces Journal International*, May 2000, pp. 30–33.